AN OREGON MESSAGE

Also by William Stafford

A Glass Face in the Rain
Stories That Could Be True
Someday, Maybe
Allegiances
The Rescued Year
Traveling Through the Dark
West of Your City

William Stafford   AN

OREGON

MESSAGE

PERENNIAL LIBRARY

Harper & Row, Publishers, New York
Cambridge, Philadelphia, San Francisco, Washington
London, Mexico City, São Paulo, Singapore, Sydney

Some of these poems appeared originally in *The Chicago Tribune, Concerning Poetry, Cornell Review, The Critical Quarterly, Field, Hampden-Sydney Poetry Review, Human Voice, Ironwood, Kansas Quarterly, Miami Magazine, The Nation, New Letters, The New Republic, Northwest Review, Poetry Northwest, Western Humanities Review, and Yankee.*

"When I Met My Muse" and "My Mother Said" were published in *The Christian Science Monitor.*

"Maybe Alone on My Bike" and "An Oregon Message" appeared originally in *The New Yorker.*

"Uncle Bill Visits" had first publication in *Poetry.*

FIRST EDITION

Designer: Sidney Feinberg

Library of Congress Cataloging-in-Publication Data

Stafford, William Edgar, 1914–
  An Oregon message.

  I. *Title.*
PS3537.T14207   1987   811'.54   87-208
ISBN 0-06-055093-7   87 88 89 90 91 MPC 10 9 8 7 6 5 4 3 2 1
ISBN 0-06-096213-5 *(pbk.)*   87 88 89 90 91 MPC 10 9 8 7 6 5 4 3 2 1

Contents

3. A WRITER'S FOUNTAIN PEN TALKING

4. SAINT MATTHEW AND ALL

5. THE BIG PICTURE

9

Some Notes on Writing

My poems are organically grown, and it is my habit to allow language its own freedom and confidence. The results will sometimes bewilder conservative readers and hearers, especially those who try to control all emergent elements in discourse for the service of predetermined ends.

Each poem is a miracle that has been invited to happen. But these words, after they come, you look at what's there. Why these? Why not some calculated careful contenders? Because these chosen ones must survive as they were made, by the reckless impulse of a fallible but susceptible person. I must be willingly fallible in order to deserve a place in the realm where miracles happen.

Writing poems is living in that realm. Each poem is a gift, a surprise that emerges as itself and is only later subjected to order and evaluation.

1 THE BOOK ABOUT YOU

Keeping a Journal

At night it was easy for me with my little candle
to sit late recording what happened that day. Sometimes
rain breathing in from the dark would begin softly
across the roof and then drum wildly for attention.
The candle flame would hunger after each wafting
of air. My pen inscribed thin shadows that leaned
forward and hurried their lines along the wall.

More important than what was recorded, these evenings
deepened my life: they framed every event
or thought and placed it with care by the others.
As time went on, that scribbled wall—even if
it stayed blank—became where everything
recognized itself and passed into meaning.

First Grade

In the play Amy didn't want to be
anybody; so she managed the curtain.
Sharon wanted to be Amy. But Sam
wouldn't let anybody be anybody else—
he said it was wrong. "All right," Steve said,
"I'll be me, but I don't like it."
So Amy was Amy, and we didn't have the play.
And Sharon cried.

A Life, a Ritual

My mother had a child, one dark
like her, but bland—wide gaze—who stared
where eternity was, then back to her eyes,
and the world. A blanket protected, a song
instructed, and the years came along, came along.

There are people whose game is success, but others
hear distance: guided, often betrayed,
they wander their lives. Their voices go by
every day, outside of history, outside
of importance. They ritual whatever they do.

My mother is nothing now. Her child—
wide gaze like hers—remembers the blanket,
and the song that taught how to lose. Oh, shadow
that came large on a wall, then face that recognized
mine: this distant song about failure

Is for you, is for you.

Surrounded by Mountains

Digging potatoes east of Sapporo
we would listen at noon to world news.

The little radio was in one of the furrows,
propped against a lunch bucket.

We didn't make any judgments. Our fields
were wide, slanting from wooded foothills.

    Religious leaders called for
    a revival of spirit in the world.

    Certain statesmen from important
    nations were considering a summit meeting.

Old Mrs. Osaka, permanently
bent over, stirred the clods beside her.

Rice fields, yellow as sunflowers,
marked off kilometers below us.

The shrine where the crows lived
had a bell that told us when rest was over.

Goodby, old friends. I remember the Prime Minister
talking, and the water jar in the shade.

Little Rooms

I rock high in the oak—secure, big branches—
at home while darkness comes. It gets lonely up here
as lights needle forth below, through airy space.
Tinkling dishwashing noises drift up, and a faint
smooth gush of air through leaves, cool evening
moving out over the earth. Our town leans farther
away, and I ride through the arch toward midnight,
holding on, listening, hearing deep roots grow.

There are rooms in a life, apart from others, rich
with whatever happens, a glimpse of moon, a breeze.
You who come years from now to this brief spell
of nothing that was mine: the open, slow passing
of time was a gift going by. I have put my hand out
on the mane of the wind, like this, to give it to you.

The Big House

She was a modern, you know.
He, you know, dealt in land.
They maintained, you know, several gardens.
You know, when the wind blows, their flowers are famous.

Their house was well built, they say.
And they say the foundation had rock under it.
Some of the walls, they say, were two feet thick.
An artist, they say, designed the door handle.

Construction took I don't know how long,
and I don't know how many bedrooms.
They needed I don't know how big a plan.
But the whole thing—I don't know how—fell down.

They're gone, they say, you know. I don't know where.

A Voice from the Past

I never intended this face, believe me,
friends; but it's hard not to be, when
history comes looking for subjects.

Others from the sixties got away somehow,
some by death, many by stealth,
and all fell away through time.

In muted bravado, I've slithered to here,
tooting a tiny horn, celebrating
what comes, being historical.

Now I pretend to belong to today,
saying my name over and over
and being my face, and sorry.

Confessions of an Individual

I let history happen—sorry. When Muslims and
Christians fought in the Crusades, I didn't stop it;
the Egyptians and Jews clashed and my efforts were not
sufficient to prevent that. Remote effects from these
disasters still exist, and I have not erased them.
My ancestors were busy cutting hay, planting potatoes,
and so on. True, they probably spent a lot of time drinking
and talking, and I let that go on for years—I can't deny it.

On the other hand, a group of people discovered wheat,
corn, smelting of iron, prevention of disease, and I didn't
help very much. Heroic actions took place, and I didn't
even take the trouble to be there.
Now I am taking the time to think about all this and
write it down. And you are taking the time to read it.

To Recite Every Day

This bread is rye. Many places,
the poor eat it, for its grain
grows anywhere and makes a gray flour.
You can eat it, or pretend.

Here are heavy shoes. They last
for years—clumsy, yes,
but they are cheap. They tramp
to work, early mornings. Put them on.

Now stand up. The old law says
work for pay. Try that shovel
or this broom, just to see
how it is, for a while.

Sleeping Toward Heaven

I wish that I had been one of the Seven Sleepers of Ephesus,
their cave was so quiet and their bed a dim century
forgotten till their return. Think of our time—
bells and honks, a schedule even for how to relax
for success. But when they woke up, their work had all
been finished—had transformed the whole world:

While they slept, faith flowered, an outside dream,
and surrounded them in their cave. All they had to do
was to sleep toward Heaven and open their eyes
like dolls. Up there on the ceiling was all they needed.

(The first line is the first sentence in *The Making of Late Antiquity*, by Peter
Brown, Harvard University Press, 1978.)

For People with Problems About How to Believe

1.

Say it's early morning, coming awake—
after a while you begin to believe. At first,
barely light, only a surmise, only a guess:
even birds doubt, but they talk to each
other. One takes the plunge and says yes.
But not quite yet—the doubters wait: gray
everywhere, nothing else, just between times.
You relax. But it gets harder to doubt.
At exactly the time when you really believe
a red-hot little arc silently slits the whole
horizon and the sun comes irresistibly into the world
and is.

2.

Or maybe this works:
you sing a little, wait—
hear that far song
coming back at you? Is it only
your ears not wanting to
be alone? They wander
deep silence and come up
with sounds made out of
need, the way puppies
learn friends—everybody
at once, wiggling to say
love is everywhere.

3.

Or on the way to Alaska you can feel those leafy
quietudes, long invitations to states

that haven't even been found. Your soul begins
to brim the horizon, ready to escape
and never come back. Later you tell people
and they won't believe you—they want the facts.
But some facts happen only to people who are ready
for how the Yukon turns over when you say its name.

4.

Sometimes you are walking: you begin
to know—even those things out of sight or hearing,
stones in the ground, flocks of birds
beyond the horizon. A little bit of snow
forms in the sky: you feel it furring
out there, ready; then it comes down.
A quality of attention has been given to you:
when you turn your head the whole world
leans forward. It waits there thirsting
after its names, and you speak it all out as it
comes to you; you go forward into forest leaves
holding out your hands, trusting all encounters,
telling every mile, "Take me home."

Next Time

Next time what I'd do is look at
the earth before saying anything. I'd stop
just before going into a house
and be an emperor for a minute
and listen better to the wind
    or to the air being still.

When anyone talked to me, whether
blame or praise or just passing time,
I'd watch the face, how the mouth
had to work, and see any strain, any
sign of what lifted the voice.

And for all, I'd know more—the earth
bracing itself and soaring, the air
finding every leaf and feather over
forest and water, and for every person
the body glowing inside the clothes
    like a light.

Burning a Book

Protecting each other, right in the center
a few pages glow a long time.
The cover goes first, then outer leaves
curling away, then spine and a scattering.
Truth, brittle and faint, burns easily,
its fire as hot as the fire lies make—
flame doesn't care. You can usually find
a few charred words in the ashes.

And some books ought to burn, trying for character
but just faking it. More disturbing
than book ashes are whole libraries that no one
got around to writing—desolate
towns, miles of unthought-in cities,
and the terrorized countryside where wild dogs
own anything that moves. If a book
isn't written, no one needs to burn it—
ignorance can dance in the absence of fire.

So I've burned books. And there are many
I haven't even written, and nobody has.

Salt Creek

It's a place to go, far in the country,
unadvertised, where even the storms pass by.
Secrets there—that nobody wants to know—
rustle away; a bridge holds in stone, with water-
sounds loud in spring and in summer low.
Deep in that golden light minnows play.
That's where I go every summer, because we lived there,
and wind, and space, and the hurt of space after
the others are gone, and my visit this one last time,
and the bittern's cry.

The Book About You

The book that tells about you slumps in the library
somewhere in the medical section. It is vague at first
but then detailed: you are hopeless and not even interesting.
Cases like yours routine through hospitals, especially
in slum districts. By the end of the book, you are dead
one-third of the time but live a useful life
occasionally if treated early. One patient
in Calcutta lived fifteen years. Softly you close
the book and push back. You walk past the travel section
and the mysteries and romances. At the door you turn for a glance:
they have established a new shelf—pay books. The librarian
is watching you. You spread your hands, go out
the quiet door, and stand there enjoying the sun.
There are days like this for everyone. Somebody else
will put the book back. Strangely—one of the symptoms?—
you feel like singing.

Thinking About Being Called Simple by a Critic

I wanted the plums, but I waited.
The sun went down. The fire
went out. With no lights on
I waited. From the night again—
those words: how stupid I was.
And I closed my eyes to listen.
The words all sank down, deep
and rich. I felt their truth
and began to live them. They were mine
to enjoy. Who but a friend
could give so sternly what the sky
feels for everyone but few learn to
cherish? In the dark with the truth
I began the sentence of my life
and found it so simple there was no way
back into qualifying my thoughts
with irony or anything like that.
I went to the fridge and opened it—
sure enough the light was on.
I reached in and got the plums.

Learning How to Lose

All your years learning how to live to win,
how others judge you, who counts—you know
it's wrong: but those habits cling that brought you
this freedom. You know how to earn it but
you don't now what it is—a friend that you
make is conquered, like an enemy.

Somewhere you'll rest, have faith, even
lose sometimes, accept the way you are, say
easily to the world: "Leave me alone, Hours.
I'm just living here. Let Now win."

Querencia

Years and miles ago in a high country
one morning the sun shone into a cave—splendid
paintings leaped into color. A mysterious artist
had worked by candlelight on the walls in secret.

Rockslides now have hidden that room. No chart
or path or tunnel penetrates, no person remembers.
All of history has turned aside from that glimpse
the sun had; nobody believes in that room anymore.

It is there.

2 SERVING WITH GIDEON

Serving with Gideon

Now I remember: in our town the druggist
prescribed Coca-Cola mostly, in tapered
glasses to us, and to the elevator
man in a paper cup, so he could
drink it elsewhere because he was black.

And now I remember The Legion—gambling
in the back room, and no women but girls, old boys
who ran the town. They were generous,
to their sons or the sons of friends.
And of course I was almost one.

I remember winter light closing
its great blue first slowly eastward
along the street, and the dark then, deep
as war, arched over a radio show
called the thirties in the great old U.S.A.

Look down, stars—I was almost
one of the boys. My mother was folding
her handkerchief; the library seethed and sparked;
right and wrong arced; and carefully
I walked with my cup toward the elevator man.

Ground Zero

A bomb photographed me on the stone,
on a white wall, a burned outline where
the bomb rays found me out in the open
and ended me, person and shadow, never to cast
a shadow again, but be here so light
the sun doesn't know. People on Main Street
used to stand in their certain chosen places—
I walk around them. It wouldn't be right
if I stood there. But all of their shadows are mine now—
I am so white on the stone.

Looking for Gold

A flavor like wild honey begins
when you cross the river. On a sandbar
sunlight stretches out its limbs, or is it
a sycamore, so brazen, so clean and bold?
You forget about gold. You stare—and a flavor
is rising all the time from the trees.
Back from the river, over by a thick
forest, you feel the tide of wild honey
flooding your plans, flooding the hours
till they waver forward looking back. They can't
return: that river divides more than
two sides of your life. The only way
is farther, breathing that country, becoming
wise in its flavor, a native of the sun.

Stillborn

Where a river touches an island
under willows leaning over
I watch the waves and think of you,
    who almost lived.

Stars will rake the sky again,
and time go on, the dark, the cold.
Clouds will race when the wind begins,
    where you almost were.

But while the thunder shakes the world
and the graceful dance and the powerful win,
still faithful, still in thought, I bow,
    little one.

Chicory

Till the great darkness gathers them in
some time in the quiet after us
they have a secret life of their own
down there near the ground, and they will go on
like those things you don't say
when someone interrupts and you
told them once, so you stop. In that long
interval those blue flowers begin to report.

Every night under my pillow the earth ticks
while somewhere in distant country tomorrow
wanders looking for me, and every morning
I go out and pat the ground again. Already
that comet with destiny in it has come by
a few times, but the years are still friendly.

Certain blue flowers hold on, hold on.

Say You Are Lonely

More still than a star, one thought shies
by: what if the sky loved you?
But nobody knew? But that magnet in space
pulled hard? But you acted like nothing at all
was reaching or calling for you? More still
than a star going by, that thought stays.
A day at a time pieces of it glow.
Nobody notices: quiet days.

Honeysuckle

Not yet old enough, still only a kid,
you meet Hazel. She is not old enough either—
it is the world before: it is early. The two of you
walk through slow, heavy, thick air.

Now you are coming to the corner where hummingbirds have
their nest. You breathe. It is the honeysuckle
tangled along the church wall. Each of you
takes a blossom to taste as you say goodby.

That flavor lasts a long time. Forever.

Scars

They tell how it was, and how time
came along, and how it happened
again and again. They tell
the slant life takes when it turns
and slashes your face as a friend.

Any wound is real. In church
a woman lets the sun find
her cheek, and we see the lesson:
there are years in that book; there are sorrows
a choir can't reach when they sing.

Rows of children lift their faces of promise,
places where the scars will be.

School Play

You were a princess, lost; I
was a little bird. Nobody cared
where we went or how we sang.
A storm, I seem to remember, a giant
wave, some kind of crash at the end.
I think we cried when they took off our wings.

If time should happen again—and it could;
we're still in a play, you know—maybe
we'll hide so well the wave will pass
and after the storm we'll come out. We both
will really believe what, even then, we knew:
not the princess, not the bird—but the song—
    was true.

A Ceremony: Doing the Needful

Carrying you, a little model carefully dressed
up, nestled on velvet in a tiny box,
I climb a mountain west of Cody. Often,
cut by snow, sheltering to get warm, I take
you out and prop you on the rocks, looking south
each time. You can see the breaks, down through cedars
to miles of tan grass. I put you back in the box
and hold you inside my coat. At the top I put you
wedged in a line of boulders, out of the wind.
It is very late by now, getting dark. I leave
you there. All the way down I can hear the earth
explaining necessity and how cold it is when you walk
away, even though you've done all you can.

Graffiti

What's on the wall will influence your life,
they say; but erasing the wall will remind
everyone what was there. So a city
is troubled for years, and one of the ways
to live is to learn how to look away.

"Kill the tyrants," lovers of mankind say,
and the religious write firmly, "Jesus saves."
"A wall for not writing on" and "I waited an hour"
are two that commuters must read. And—remember?—
Daniel Boone carved "kilt a bar" on a tree.

But the trees not carved and walls undefaced
mean "Not even Kilroy was here,"
and millions of us haven't killed anyone,
or a bear, or even an hour. We haven't
presumed. And—who knows?—maybe we're saved.

For the Unknown Enemy

This monument is for the unknown
good in our enemies. Like a picture
their life began to appear: they
gathered at home in the evening
and sang. Above their fields they saw
a new sky. A holiday came
and they carried the baby to the park
for a party. Sunlight surrounded them.

Here we glimpse what our minds long turned
away from. The great mutual
blindness darkened that sunlight in the park,
and the sky that was new, and the holidays.
This monument says that one afternoon
we stood here letting a part of our minds
escape. They came back, but different.
Enemy: one day we glimpsed your life.

This monument is for you.

Being an American

Some network has bought history, all the rights
for wars and games. At home the rest of us
wait. Nothing happens, of course.
We know that somewhere our times are
alive and flashing, for real. We sigh.
If we had been rich we could have lived
like that. Maybe even yet we could buy
a little bit of today and see how it is.

Our Time

It came when autumn came, the right day,
so clear and gold it shook us like a storm:
what the world promised had come, and we were
afraid. It was so late a year, even though the right one.

We didn't need any stars, only trees
with tops that leaned and on the roads
cars held near the ground by wheels
too sure and round for the young.

We knew no harm would come, stopped by miles
and luck, with serene hills to stand
right where they did the most good. Hills
are like that sometimes, near, to help.

No need, except for time, only a little space
to turn and move, as if calmly, on,
steady, past leaves, past hills and roads,
where we were going—away, and the end of the world.

Over the North Jetty

Geese and brant, their wingbeat
steady—it's a long flight, Alaska—
bank their approach and then curve
upwind for landing. They live where storms
are so usual they are almost fair weather.

And we lean in that permanent gale,
watching those cold flocks depend on their wings
as they veer out of the north. In the last flight
one laggard pulls farther downwind
and peels off to disappear alone in the storm.

If you follow an individual away like that
a part of your life is lost forever,
beating somewhere in darkness, and belonging
only to storms that haunt around the world
on that risky path just over the wave.

On Earth

Any sun that comes, even
one not ours, could have these lakes
to drink out of, any time.

And other laws could come besides
the ones we have, all springing
from a force that makes them right.

The lives we have, while we have them,
can measure time, before and after
today, to use or give away.

On earth it is like this, a strange
gift we hold, while we look around.

Walking with Your Eyes Shut

Your ears receive a platter of sound
heaped where you are, in the center, verging
off at far edges that move as you pass,
like a great hoopskirt of listening through the world.
A brick wall compresses your right ear's horizon
on that side, but the whole sound sky balloons
again all around. A cardinal's whistle
soars up and arcs down behind you. A blue jay
unrolls its part of the day, a long streamer over you,
and then little discs receding smaller and
smaller into the infinity that lives
in the middle of the woods beyond. You carry
this dome all the time. Today you know it,
a great rich room, a musical sky.

A Dream of Descartes

When dawn comes along any morning it carries
a thin, faint message falling from unearthly
height all the way into the world—
how north from here waits a forest, and north
from there a storm that will never stop,
more arctic than zero, sending those knives of cold.

And you begin to know—things that happen
clash; they sound in the real wind, but
beyond them come forms: whimpering evasions
muffled but there, wars we didn't
have, epidemics where heroes died
except that they didn't happen, the years
left out of time, our walls we didn't
build, and—spaced all the way to forever—
our inexhaustible inheritance, Pride and Ignorance.

When You Hear This

1.

When you hear this I am twenty
years old. Though I do not know it,
all the flowers are on my side.
When I go along the street, every
color—a house, the sky, a tree—
hits deep into my life
where sounds are already celebrating.
You come along, twenty. Together
we get into the Santa Maria and sail
straight on past the edge of the world.

2.

When you hear this, remember that girl
you passed when the light was changing.
She was brave, but you saw
a shadow leaning toward her
across the street. In her hands
was a folder—directions for finding
this way of looking at her, a strange
double way of being someone else
by lending yourself for a moment,
as you have just done.

3.

When you hear this you should
turn it around in your thought,
then squint your eyes. Later
there will be a quiz about this.
Before finishing you should think
barefoot on the sand at the beach,

the scuffing. Do that. Now the
feel of the wind when it presses you back
from the cliff edge and then reverses.
Only one more thing before
the end: you should always return
to yourself after a dream,
as you have just done.

Waiting in Line

You the very old, I have come
to the edge of your country and looked across,
how your eyes warily look into mine
when we pass, how you hesitate when
we approach a door. Sometimes
I understand how steep your hills
are, and your way of seeing the madness
around you, the careless waste of the calendar,
the rush of people on buses. I have
studied how you carry packages,
balancing them better, giving them attention.
I have glimpsed from within the gray-eyed look
at those who push, and occasionally even I
can achieve your beautiful bleak perspective
on the loud, the inattentive, shoving boors
jostling past you toward their doom.

With you, from the pavement I have watched
the nation of the young, like jungle birds
that scream as they pass, or gyrate on playgrounds,
their frenzied bodies jittering with the disease
of youth. Knowledge can cure them. But
not all at once. It will take time.

There have been evenings when the light
has turned everything silver, and like you
I have stopped at a corner and suddenly
staggered with the grace of it all: to have
inherited all this, or even the bereavement
of it and finally being cheated!—the chance
to stand on a corner and tell it goodby!

Every day, every evening, every
abject step or stumble has become heroic:—

You others, we the very old have a country.
A passport costs everything there is.

Not Having Wings

If I had a wing it might hurt,
be broken. I would trail it
around, stumbling on it. Maybe infection
sets in. Tortured by terrible pain,
I forget all about God and curse
and am lost. I'm glad I don't have any wings.

Now when I hobble, it is an act
of mercy for that knee, the one
relied on so often in the sugar-beet fields.
I get somewhere; I relax, letting
me and the rest of the world balance
again: Take it easy, World, old friend.

Afterward

In the day I sheltered on the sunny side
of big stones. In the whole world other things
were giddy: they moved. I leaned on the steady part.

Every day passed into darkness. Dawn
rescued the top of the rocks and the middle
and then me. The sun loved my face.

You can hardly believe what I did: when winter
came, when the nights began to be cold,
I dissolved away into the still part of the world.

Now it is cold and dark, and the long nights
return to the wilderness. One big rock is here
for my place. All else moves. I am learning to wait.

Four Oak Leaves

1.

When I was green, everyone loved me. Bees
crooned my sweetness; butterflies made me their own.
But then something called time began to drag me
away and I became curled up and brittle and brown.

2.

These lines you read are what an oak leaf wrote,
following a storm that dragged it over the snow—
complaining and kicking. "I don't want to forsake
my tree. Help! Where did my sisters go?"

3.

When spring comes, a whole new cast will have the stage
and I will huddle where winter threw me away,
but wherever I am the soil will be bitter because
I remember how lonely it was when I tried to stay.

4.

This farewell comes from a forgiving leaf
that skipped with the others and then found a lucky storm
that brought me here. Listen—hold on as long
as you can, then trust forth: make truth your home.

An Oregon Message

When we first moved here, pulled
the trees in around us, curled
our backs to the wind, no one
had ever hit the moon—no one.
Now our trees are safer than the stars,
and only other people's neglect
is our precious and abiding shell,
pierced by meteors, radar, and the telephone.

From our snug place we shout
religiously for attention, in order to hide:
only silence or evasion will bring
dangerous notice, the hovering hawk
of the state, or the sudden quiet stare
and fatal estimate of an alerted neighbor.

This message we smuggle out in
its plain cover, to be opened
quietly: Friends everywhere—
we are alive! Those moon rockets
have missed millions of secret
places! Best wishes.

Burn this.

Why I Am Happy

Now has come, an easy time. I let it
roll. There is a lake somewhere
so blue and far nobody owns it.
A wind comes by and a willow listens
gracefully.

I hear all this, every summer. I laugh
and cry for every turn of the world,
its terribly cold, innocent spin.
That lake stays blue and free; it goes
on and on.

And I know where it is.

3 A WRITER'S FOUNTAIN PEN TALKING

Bird Count

Choose a day: whatever birds come,
they're the ones, for this year.
If it's windy, multiply by two. (But what
if there's none, but might be? Mark *none*.)
Today there may be a song. Multiply:
"Two unknowns." But you are always
the same, no matter how windy or cold
it is. You search all the thickets, then walk
home through the fields at the end: just one.

A Day at Home

On the near pine rain hangs
the way I suppose it hangs
on the far.

Being yourself, you are always
on time—right where your kind
of person should be.

Why not wait here while the rest
of the world happens? It is better as
history than it is as news.

The dog, his head on the coffee table,
gazes tranquilly, resting his chin
on a volume of Martin Buber.

The Dean at Faculty Retreat

They go by, dragging their chains. I hook
to each a little rubber band and slip
the tether to a stake at the end. They go on
but after a time their heads turn. They
stop. Slowly I walk toward them
talking quietly and calling their names.
On their necks I hang their slogan, any color
they like: "Freedom," fastened to the chain.

Final Exam: American Renaissance

Fill in blanks: Your name is
_____ _____ldo Emerson. Your friend
Thor_____ lives at _____Pond; he owes
you rent and an ax. Your
neighbor in a house with_____ gables
won't respond to another neighbor, Herman
_____, who broods about a whale colored _____.
You think it is time for America to _____.

In a few choice words, tell why.

The Rodeo at Sisters, Oregon

When the speaker stops we can hear
the mountains not saying anything.

The nails in this grandstand
are better than the boards.

Indians make the best cowboys.

One of the riders put his brand
on a Cadillac.

The meanest horses ride the best trailers.

In this country, no swagger, but sometimes
you look it when you almost fall.

About the time a rope gets to feeling good
it breaks.

One of the broncs is champion here, but
the prizes go to riders.

Some of the judges can ride
but they don't need that kind of money.

Prize money is hard to keep—most
dollars hurry right back to Las Vegas.

Simple Talk

Spilling themselves in the sun bluebirds
wing-mention their names all day. If everything
told so clear a life, maybe the sky would
come, maybe heaven; maybe appearance and
truth would be the same. Maybe whatever seems
to be so, we should speak so from our souls,
never afraid, "Light" when it comes,
"Dark" when it goes away.

Purifying the Language of the Tribe

Walking away means
"Goodby."

Pointing a knife at your stomach means
"Please don't say that again."

Leaning toward you means
"I love you."

Raising a finger means
"I enthusiastically agree."

"Maybe" means
"No."

"Yes" means
"Maybe."

Looking like this at you means
"You had your chance."

Starting with Little Things

Love the earth like a mole,
fur-near. Nearsighted,
hold close the clods,
their fine-print headlines.
Pat them with soft hands—

But spades, but pink and loving: they
break rock, nudge giants aside,
affable plow.
Fields are to touch:
each day nuzzle your way.

Tomorrow the world.

Today

Somebody today called me "old."
I whirled: "Why, you
young whippersnapper!"

"See, Pop—that's what I mean: you
called me 'young' and
'whippersnapper'! See, Pop?"

Why, that . . . "Wait," I called, "now
wait just a little minute," but that imp
scampered around out of reach and laughed.

I lunged—I'm not that old—and had him.
He twisted, and I saw him familiar—
he was like me, just such a scamp.

"What have you done with the rest of my life!"
And he looked so scared, just like me,
that I didn't want to know.

And I let him go,
and he ran.

Ultimate Problems

In the Aztec design God crowds
into the little pea that is rolling
out of the picture.
All the rest extends bleaker
because God has gone away.

In the White Man design, though,
no pea is there.
God is everywhere,
but hard to see.
The Aztecs frown at this.

How do you know He is everywhere?
And how did He get out of the pea?

Uncle Bill Visits

Remember me, kids? Here:
My head a high pumpkin, to you I take off
the lid. I reach with my hand and take
the vine handle—so. Look!—these gropy
little seeds inside want summers and rain,
open hillsides and many long furrows
in fields full of Halloween dreams.

Here's where the fire lives, here, to shine
out of my eyes. Watch out for the flame!—
I have brought empires down to squeaks in
the weeds; weasels have hidden here, and saints.
I folded Rome here. And, yes, there are
boxes I wouldn't want to disturb.

In this room I built a glass eye with camera
inside, linked with Telstar: remember the blind
old beggar you passed on the way to the movies?—
he broadcast by Telstar the whole mardi gras
your town plays; and once when you clattered
a nickel, one day in his cup, it deafened
the scanners tuned up for subtler acts,
all the way back to the echoing halls of
the Pentagon.

Oh, there are too many acts, children, we
grownups know. I could tell you about
a world where fathers and mothers are
lost, and their children might save them.
But now, my head a high pumpkin, I reach up

my hand and put the lid with the vine handle
firmly down again—so. Now go tell your parents
Uncle Bill's come.

Visiting

1.
The weather visits us. It has another
cup. Down by the barn, it waves.

2.
Like that you'll find me someday.
Not now—no need to look.

3.
You'll feel a touch again—your hair, a slap
on the back. Just once.

4.
Clouds do a still-day dance called "Disappear":
they don't move—they're gone,

5.
And that's how I won't move too. We'll have days,
then comes that day: So long.

Volkswagen

I heard that un-engine in front
not caring all the way up the mountain,
like your love letters not in
my suitcase when I left home for college.

Listen, the war is behind us,
and men have invented a car for
all, with a place in front where
we might still put love letters.

When I Met My Muse

I glanced at her and took my glasses
off—they were still singing. They buzzed
like a locust on the coffee table and then
ceased. Her voice belled forth, and the
sunlight bent. I felt the ceiling arch, and
knew that nails up there took a new grip
on whatever they touched. "I am your own
way of looking at things," she said. "When
you allow me to live with you, every
glance at the world around you will be
a sort of salvation." And I took her hand.

Where the Saw Is

It waits in its little room. You turn
a key and it comes awake. Trembling,
it yells at a touch. When they hear it
the trees fall down. God waits
while the motor is running. A little
taste, and air follows the blade.
It calls everyone "Mister."
Even heroes, even tigers, better leave it alone.

Ghalib Decides to Be Reticent

There is a question I would like to ask
the world. But I don't think I will ever ask it.

Strange to think—I have thought too far
and now must hide a discovery.

I couldn't make the world, or even change it,
but I can find something here and keep it before I go.

Friends, if you knew what I'm talking about
you would be glad that I didn't tell you.

A Writer's Fountain Pen Talking

I gave out one day and left a woman
tied to a railroad track.

And what happened next?

The train couldn't go on; it stopped with a
foot in the air, like Napoleon's horse on the bridge
when it knew the plank was gone.

What ever happened?

When they filled the pen again—this was years later—
the train backed up, and an old woman
climbed on: she had waited all that time
to be rescued, or killed. She felt cheated,
for that strange diversion.

Where is she now?

Right here on this page, hiding in the ink you see.

Stone, Paper, Scissors

Stone
> You put your hand on stone, for the coolness there,
> and how steady. It hasn't the wit of water, but you trust
> it more. It will be there again tomorrow,
> earning its place by not being anything else.
> Remember the story of the bat?—hollering into
> a cave, "Anybody there?" and a big rock
> saying, "Nobody but me," and the others, "But me," "But me,"
> till the whole mountain had answered. That's how a rock is.

Paper
> Paper is always ready: "Where shall we go?"
> "Anywhere." It will cover stone, but it has
> no principles. "You like melodrama?" "Sure."
> "And how about dullness?" "Great!" "But what is your best
> friend?" "Well, I don't know . . ." it wanders on.
> It seems agreeable but it may be guiding
> you just by being so flat and letting you
> relax all the time. But it can cover stone.

Scissors
> Scissors? That's different. It breaks on rock,
> but it knows exactly where paper goes, and it bites
> right where paper is. "What is the worth
> of this story?" "Not much," scissors says. And it closes
> its mouth on the truth, making it into many.
> Scissors, paper, stone—how are they like us?—
> what do they show? Each of them needs a friend.

83

The Sparkle Depends on Flaws
in the Diamond

Wood that can learn is no good for a bow.

The eye that can stand the sun can't
    see in shadow.

Fish don't find the channel—the channel
    finds them.

If the root doesn't trust, the plant
    won't blossom,

A dog that knows jaguars is no longer
    useful in hunting.

You can lie at a banquet, but you have to
    be honest in the kitchen.

A Day Last Summer

"Cowbird," someone said. I was
biggest in the nest, and looked around—
we're all gaping our beaks (mine
the highest), and our mother fluttering
her little yellow wings and cheeping
because these people carrying binoculars
had stopped and were peering at us, our place
in the low hawthorn. "Look at that"—
I turned as far as I could, but it was
just us—"look at that damn greedy
giant." But then I caught the first
bug our mother brought, and oh it
was so good! I gulped. I loved
my brothers and sisters and bustling mother.
The people went away and I bawled, "More!
More!" And it was so beautiful a day.

Mr. or Mrs. Nobody

Some days when you look out, the land
is heavy, following its hills, dim
where a road bends. There are days when
having the world is a mistake.
But then you think, "Well, anyway, it wasn't
my idea," and its OK again.

Suppose that a person who knows you happens
to see you going by, and it's one of those days—
for a minute you have to carry the load
for them, you've got to lift the whole
heavy world, even without knowing it,
being a hero, stumbling along.
Some days it's like that. And maybe
today. And maybe all of the time.

Ode to Garlic

Sudden, it comes for you
in the cave of yourself where you know
and are lifted by important events.

Say you are dining and it happens:
soaring like an eagle, you are
pierced by a message from the midst of life:

Memory—what holds the days together—touches
your tongue. It is from deep in the earth
and it reaches out kindly, saying, "Hello, Old Friend."

It make us alike, all offspring of powerful
forces, part of one great embrace of democracy,
united across every boundary.

You walk out generously, giving it back
in a graceful wave, what you've been given.
Like a child again, you breathe on the world, and it shines.

4 SAINT MATTHEW AND ALL

Scripture

In the dark book where words crowded together,
a land with spirits waited, and they rose and walked
every night when the book opened by candlelight—

A sacred land where the words touched the trees
and their leaves turned into fire. We carried it wherever
we went, our hidden scene; and in the sigh of snow coming down,

In the city sometimes a people without any book
drove tunneling by in traffic, eyes measuring
chances ahead, the red light at the end of the block—

Then sprung over that city a dark word like judgment
arched, every face turned into a soul
wandering the shadow of the tabernacle world.

Forget

Forget the rain, being inside,
and the sound, how the windows darkened,
or running outside, boats of leaves
launched for a dangerous race in the gutter.

Forget Sister singing to her doll
in the corner, devotion forever to all
her children, and offering half of any
gift to her brother, or anyone.

Forget the town, surrounded by the world,
shadowed by giants who would always answer
your questions—Where did we come from? Who
will take care of us all when the next time comes?

Forget those figures in white sheets and Father
saying, "I think that one is Grundy"—
and shivering and wondering, "What kind of people
are they? Why does my father shrink away?"

Forget that band on Main, the limping
man, the singers with tambourines
in fair or stormy weather, saying,
"Repent!" and "Lest ye burn!"

Forget.

Turn Over Your Hand

Those lines on your palm, they can be read
for a hidden part of your life that only
those links can say—nobody's voice
can find so tiny a message as comes
across your hand. Forbidden to complain,
you have tried to be like somebody else,
and only this fine record you examine
sometimes like this can remember where
you were going before that long
silent evasion that your life became.

Pilgrims

They come to the door, usually carrying or leading
a child, always with The Book held between them
and the world. They quote Ezekiel, Daniel, Kings.
They look at us and think of Nebuchadnezzar
eating the grass. It is good to listen, because
maybe they are angels, and behind them the sky arches,
the trees glisten in worship of the sun.

These travelers in the Word and their offspring have
their commission from somewhere, filtered down, through
mistakes, pride, greed, and the plans committees
make, the way pilgrims have always come.
Over their shoulders day extends its hand;
beside them a child whimpers. It bows its head
as we bow: it hungers; it cries; it will be fed.

1932

Nobody could come because ours was the house
with the quarantine sign in red, "Scarlet Fever."
We looked out through the tree that whispered all night
its green "Life, life in the world."

Others had school. They would live. They
could run past every day and not look.
At night we listened for stars, and we talked
of miles we would go sometime if our house
let us out, if the doctor ever said yes.

When they took the sign down it was over,
but we carried a lesson the stars had brought,
those times when people turned away.

1940

It is August. Your father is walking you
to the train for camp and then the War
and on out of his life, but you don't know.

Little lights along the path glow under their hoods
and your shoes go brown, brown in the brightness
till the next interval, when they disappear in the shadow.

You know they are down there, by the crunch of stone
and a rustle when they touch a fern. Somewhere above,
cicadas arch their gauze of sound all over town.

Shivers of summer wind follow across the park
and then turn back. You walk on toward
September, the depot, the dark, the light, the dark.

A Game and a Brother

Afraid, but not really afraid, we heard
a step on the stair—Daddy? A ghost?
Whatever the game, here came the whole world—

But never to mean again what made
it extend so far, that way of trembling:
no one now can make me believe.

This life of mine only a present scene
turning into a past scene, I
keep trying for content in my days,

Looking around for heroes or villains,
calling out, "Maybe that's one!" But they stand
staring back ever so hard;

So I go running away, playing the game,
pretending it's that big world again,
but not believing. Bob, it's just me—

I tried. I tried.

Brother

Somebody came to the door that night.
"Where is your son, the one with the scar?"
No moon has ever shone so bright.

A bridge, a dark figure, and then the train—
"My son went away. I can't help you."
Many a clear night since then. And rain.

I was the younger, the one with the blood.
"You better tell Lefty what his brother done."
They went off cursing down the road.

A boy in the loft watching a star.
"Son, your big brother has saved your life."
He never came back, the one with the scar.

Waiting Sometimes

Inside your hands when you clasp them while waiting
a committee or appointment, you feel a warm
little room, dark, where in its own quiet
the truth is at home, recognizing itself.

Your fingers nestle communion, forgiving
each other, a lacing together of independent
beings. They even forget which hand they belong to,
and one of them volunteers to rest on the table.

The arrival of the boss or whoever is chairing
the meeting breaks up that little church;
your fingers come out in the big room, while your hands
wave hello from their warm part of the world.

Madge

Or you could do it, the speech I mean
at the end, after we come back and sit down
and look at each other. You could stare
into the fire, getting ready, then begin:
"Why did we pay any attention to her?
At the last you could see her—a shell created
by our habit of deferring, one long complaint
secretly wanting to be stopped. Brutality
could have saved her." You stir the fire.

Or I could do it, since no one else,
really, knew her that well. But my habit
of silence would stop me. Not yet could I
slouch down, put by feet up the way she never
liked, and begin to talk out the tangle
our lives had become. I would sweep the hearth:
"Did you see the flowers from the neighbors? All those
roses? And I liked what Josie said,
about the years." I'd stare at the fire.

Or, carefully, we both could say it: "She's gone."

Hearing the Song

My father said, "Listen," and that subtle song
"Coyote" came to us: we heard it together.
The river slid by, its weight
moving like oil. "It comes at night,"
he said; "some people don't like it." "It sounds
dark," I said, "like midnight, a cold . . ."
His hand pressed my shoulder:
"Just listen." That's how I first heard the song.

108 East Nineteenth

Mother, the sweet peas have gushed out of
the ground where you fell, where you lay that day
when the doctor came, while your wash kept flapping
on the line across the backyard. I stood
and looked out a long time toward the Fairgrounds.
The Victrola in the living room used to play
"Nola," and the room spun toward a center
that our neighborhood clustered around. Nasturtiums
you put in our salad would brighten our tummies,
you said, and we careened off like trains
to play tag in alfalfa fields till the moon
came out and you called us home with "Popcorn
for all who come." But that was long
before you said, "Jesus is calling me home."

And Father, when your summons came and you quietly
left, no one could hold you
back. You didn't need to talk
because your acts for years had already prayed.
For you both, may God guide my hand in its pious
act, from far off, across this page.

Mother's Day

Peg said, "This one," and we bought it
for Mother, our allowance for weeks
paid out to a clerk who snickered—
a hideous jar, oil-slick in color,
glass that light got lost in.

We saw it for candy, a sign for
our love. And it lasted:
the old house on Eleventh,
a dim room on Crescent where
the railroad shook the curtains,
that brief glory at Aunt Mabel's place.

Peg thought it got more beautiful,
Egyptian, sort of, a fire-sheened
relic. And with a doomed grasp
we carried our level of aesthetics
with us across Kansas, proclaiming
our sentimental badge.

Now Peg says, "Remember that candy jar?"
She smoothes the silver. "Mother
hated it." I am left standing
alone by the counter, ready to buy what
will hold Mother by its magic, so
she will never be mad at us again.

Getting Scared

Tending our fire in the oil drum, we felt
that second earthquake begin. Near dawn it was,
when everything stills. To be safe, we had
slept in a field. We felt a long slow wave
in the earth. It wasn't the stars that moved, but ourselves,
in time to a dance the dead could feel. Our fire
stirred where it cooled. Sparks whirled up.
Crawling along by a breath at a time, we tried to
get low; we tried to sight across level earth
near dawn and let the time tell us about how
to be alive in the grass, the miles, the strangeness,
with only the sun looking back from the other end of light.
We moved out as far as we could. "Forever," we thought,
"if we breathe too hard it will all be gone."
We spread our arms out wide on the ground
and held still. We set out for that cave we knew
above a stream, where early sunlight reaches
far back, willows all around, and clams in the river
for the taking. And we prayed for that steady event
we had loved so long without knowing it, our greatest
possession—the world when it didn't move.

A Memorial for My Mother

For long my life left hers. It went
among strangers; it weakened and followed
foreign ways, even honesty, and courage. It found
those most corrupting of all temptations,
friends—their grace, their faithfulness.

But now my life has come back. In our bleak
little town I taste salt and smoke again.
I turn into our alley and lean
where I hid from work or from anything
deserving of praise. Mother, you and I—

We knew if they knew our hearts they would blame.
We knew we deserved nothing. I go along
now being no one, and remembering this—
how alien we were from others, how hard we chewed
on our town's tough rind. How we loved its flavor.

The Land Between the Rivers

It happened to be Thursday. No one was going
to notice if I stopped by home. Anyway,
now it was gone, covered by the lake that
came, and marked with a plaque by the new road.

Here's where the house would be if I
had a son, if we owned the land, if the lake
hadn't come. I tossed a rock in the air
for all that couldn't ever be, this time.

You know the power that falls through a wire
when a river falls? How it wears for years
through its canyon? How you often come back alone?
How it turned into spray where it hit the stone?

Our Neighborhood

Sam's Mother
>   Mornings they used to
>   wheel her out over the brown
>   leaves to watch us play.

In the Album
>   One of the sad things—
>   our awards, a now-so-lonely
>   whistle in the dark.

The Quiet House
>   That's Mrs. Brown's. Her
>   son was so bad he ran away
>   and joined the navy.

The Woman Next Door
>   "She went to Vassar"—
>   my mother scrubbed on— "a school
>   where they ride horses."

How It Is with Family

Let's assume you have neglected to write
a brother or a sister. The closeness you had for years
is gone. But now there's a need—let's assume
it's about money or something. You still know
them so well you feel right about it. You begin,
and even if they don't respond, your words and the whole
idea go along as part of the world: you don't have to
be correct. You say, "It's Bob," "It's Peg," "I'm just
writing them." Let's assume someone blames
you—the reaching out as if no time had passed.
You're surprised: there's a part of the way things are
that calculating people can't know. You don't
waste much time following out that strangeness, you
just write, "Bob," or "Peg," "It's me—send the money."

When You Go Anywhere

This passport your face (not you
officially, your picture, but the face
used to make the passport) offers
everyone its witness: "This is me."

It feels like only a picture, a passport
forced upon you. Somewhere this oval,
sudden and lasting, appeared. It happened
that you were behind it, like it or not.

You present it—your passport, your face—
wherever you go. It says, "A little country,"
it says, "Allow this observer
quiet passage," it says, "Ordinary," it says, "Please."

By Tens

In my twenties the days came with a war wind
buffeting buildings and signs. Whole forests learned
their primitive gestures all over again and whined
for help. Finally the storm overwhelmed mankind.

In my thirties a lake of wisdom began
its years of expansion. To promises it answered, "When?"
And it grew by tributaries that would run
whenever my blunders brought rebukes from anyone.

In my forties a smog began to cover
the world. At first it stayed down on the level,
then it climbed. It sought out leaders wherever
a leader was. It changed the world forever.

In my fifties people began to move
away from each other. Roads we traveled were of
divergent claims. A sunset, even, would arrive
differently on successive nights of our lives.

In my sixties all that the years have brought
begins to shine—friends, the lake of wisdom,
the kindly curtain of smog where leaders are hidden,
and this path of knowing that leads us all toward heaven.

Afraid of the Dust

Afraid of the dust, closely peering
at fragments, we go cautiously among
little things, finer and finer, till no one
is able to find us and we can follow
where the labyrinth wants us to go. Oh, do you
remember when the days were fastened to wheels
of a wagon and the sun waited for the mailman?
You put your hand on the ice they swept
from the delivery truck, and summer reeled back,
nailed again. They'll never catch us now—
our town grabbed those years, and we ran and ran.
Listen—Paul went to jail, Mary
died in Denver below the tracks.
But our best summer has broken loose: it orbits
in the sky flickering over and over
its blind signal, Mary holding out again
a butterfly wing and a dime and an agate,
saying what proved to be true, "They're for you,
they're forever."

Good Room

In this best room, only a kitchen,
touch cloth—in towels—touch
metal stove, wood cupboards.
Look down the breadboard: scars
time never needs to overcome.

The easy refrigerator door closes like this:
"Forgive." Inside, a light goes to sleep
comfortably, friend of lettuce, admired
by the eggs; and the meditative motor
suggests winter, then pauses all night.

Room that gives life, alone with independent
spices content just to be in their jars:
while we live may your way be ours.
May we never forget your order, the various
world brought by recipes to anyone's taste—

The work of many made into one home.

My Mother Said

All day, deep in the mine,
miners carry a bird,
and they always watch the cage.
If the little bird still sings,
they hack and shovel, dirty and loud.

But away down there in the ground
a sudden quiet comes,
for something is terribly wrong—
the strong miners pale
and run and stumble and crawl—
if the bird withholds its song.

To the Children at the Family Album

Across Grandmother Ingersoll's face
the Civil War happened. Events crisscrossed
her mouth; and the names of battles would
stir in her eyes, herself part slave, part
free (like me, children, like you—our mouth
hers but our mind running freedom road).

Those days back home they got the moon's
report across Iowa: deportment
of corn shocks—feathers or corn leaf?—
and oak with its fingers out in vain
to hold nothing, then sigh. All that
frozen country went under, winter
only a sound, the pond a kettledrum.

Children, events can find any face,
and many as leaves are, a little weight
at last will make them fall. A hand
that reaches with love can hurt
any dear face in the world,
as love raked across the Civil War
and into the face of Grandmother Ingersoll.

What If We Were Alone?

What if there weren't any stars?
What if only the sun and the earth
circled alone in the sky? What if
no one ever found anything outside
this world right here?—no Galileo
could say, "Look—it is out there,
a hint of whether we are everything."

Look out at the stars. Yes—cold
space. Yes, we are so distant that
the mind goes hollow to think it.
But something is out there. Whatever
our limits, we are led outward. We glimpse
company. Each glittering point of light
beckons: "There is something beyond."

The moon rolls through the trees, rises
from them, and waits. In the river all
night a voice floats from rock
to sandbar, to log. What kind of listening
can follow quietly enough? We bow, and
the voice that falls through the rapids
calls all the rocks by their secret names.

Saint Matthew and All

Lorene—we thought she'd come home. But
it got late, and then days. Now
it has been years. Why shouldn't she,
if she wanted? I would: something comes
along, a sunny day, you start walking;
you meet a person who says, "Follow me,"
and things lead on.

Usually, it wouldn't happen, but sometimes
the neighbors notice your car is gone, the
patch of oil in the driveway, and it fades.
They forget.

In the Bible it happened—fishermen, Levites.
They just went away and kept going. Thomas,
away off in India, never came back.

But Lorene—it was a stranger maybe, and he
said, "Your life, I need it." And nobody else did.

5 THE

BIG

PICTURE

Run Before Dawn

Most mornings I get away, slip out
the door before light, set forth on the dim, gray
road, letting my feet find a cadence
that softly carries me on. Nobody
is up—all alone my journey begins.

Some days it's escape: the city is burning
behind me, cars have stalled in their tracks,
and everybody is fleeing like me but some other direction.
My stride is for life, a far place.

Other days it is hunting: maybe some game will cross
my path and my stride will follow for hours, matching
all turns. My breathing has caught the right beat
for endurance; familiar trancelike scenes glide by.

And sometimes it's a dream of motion, streetlights coming near,
passing, shadows that lean before me, lengthened
then fading, and a sound from a tree: a soul, or an owl.

These journeys are quiet. They mark my days with adventure
too precious for anyone else to share, little gems
of darkness, the world going by, and my breath, and the road.

Owls at the Shakespeare Festival

How do owls find each other
in the world? They fly the forest
calling, "Darling, Darling."

Each time the sun goes out a world
comes true again, for owls:
trees flame their best color—dark.

At Shakespeare once, in Ashland,
when Lear cried out, two owls
flared past the floodlights:

On my desk I keep a feather
for those far places thought
fluttered when I began to know.

Loyalty

Some people, they tire of their dog, they
get a divorce. Their car breaks down,
they trade it in. A sweater gets a hole
in the elbow, they throw it away:—

*I take thee, Rover, for better, for
worse, in sickness and in health, for
richer, for poorer, till death do us part.*

Figuring Out How It Is

How it tilts while you are thinking,
and then you know. How it makes no difference
for a long time—then it does.

How you walk along and you can't explain it
but suddenly a field from years ago
is present again, this time with its meaning.

How snow—without any power, and in its blindness
only repeating the same thing again and
again—captures mountains, whole countries.

How when a scene comes you look
over your shoulder and it's what you thought
it was but you are somebody else.

How the trees keep on, and through every summer
climb up where they are, a world better
than ours, more serene, going on forever.

How your town climbs through the clouds for years
till it can last, and you hold it there,
yours, in the sun that was always there.

How who you are made a difference once
but the wind blew, changing everything
gradually to here, and it is today.

Looking Up at Night

It's awful stillness the moon feels, how the earth
wants it, that great, still, steady rock
floating serenely around. It knows it belongs
nearer its bright neighbor that shepherds it through
the sky. And the two begin to converge toward
the docking that will shatter history and bring new continents
hissing out of the sea, and erase with tide
and sand the old eternal cities and monuments and mountains.

Dear Sky

This note is to explain after my death, if there is anyone left, what I was trying to do.

Toward the last I was protecting my friends by my careful indifference. Oh, I greeted them, and acted as usual, but I didn't let on what I felt—that terrible tide of knowing that came to me.

You, Sky, are so far that I felt sorry for you, and I began to know that all of us are lost—everyone just as lonely. It is all the way through the universe to reach anyone.

And I began to leave, so I could stand it.

Now it is cold where I live—rain. Few come near—nobody comes. And everything keeps to a separate way. When the winds go over they all talk of one storm that they plan someday. Even if anyone thought of me now, and of those other times, no one would care, this far.

But I send this note, Dear Sky. I love you, Sky.

Your friend,
A Cloud

Barnum and Bailey

And also besides, listen, in addition, there was
parked beyond the elephants a wagon with pictures on both
sides where she lived, the woman with the legs, captive
to the lion tamer, that cruel man with a chair
　　　and a mustache.

The woman with the legs was washing her hair in sunshine
when we peeked through a hole in the canvas around
their wagon. The mustache man lazily was flipping
a whip at a painted barrel in the golden light.

Listen—you never know in your life when Heaven
will come. It has to be chance. And you never get back.

Lie Detector

You said it beats like a fist, proclaiming
the truth all the time, hidden but always
there, an emblem of what we need,
a picture of how we are, slinking
in honesty, frank as our hands
or face, acting the self, helplessly true.

At night, no one else near, you walk
past fields, or trees, wind beginning
its quest, a few stars glittering,
an owl at home in the dark alone
with its name—and your heart marching along
with you, saying, "Now," saying, "Yes,"
        saying, "Here."

Deciding

One mine the Indians worked had
gold so good they left it there
for God to keep.

At night sometimes you think
your way that far, that deep,
or almost.

You hold all things or not, depending
not on greed but whether they suit what
life begins to mean.

Like those workers you study what moves,
what stays. You bow, and then, like them,
you know—

What's God, what's world, what's gold.

Help from History

Please help me know it happened,
    that life I thought we had—

    Our friends holding out their hands
        to us—
    Our enemies mistaken, infected by
        unaccountable prejudice—
    Our country benevolent, a model
        for all governments, good-willed—
    Those mad rulers at times elsewhere,
        inhuman and yet mob-worshipped,
        leaders of monstrous doctrine, unspeakable
        beyond belief, yet strangely attractive to
        the uninstructed.

And please let me believe these incredible
    legends that have dignified our lives—

    The wife or husband helplessly loving us,
        the children full of awe and affection,
        the dog insanely faithful—
    Our growing up hard—hard times, being
        industrious and reliable—
    The places we lived arched full of
        serene golden light—

Now, menaced my judgments, overheard revisions,
    let me retain what ignorance it takes
    to preserve what we need—
    a past that redeems any future.

Austere Hope, Daily Faith

Even a villain sleeps—atrocities
are intermittent. We assume few saints
among us—and inattention or fatigue
is what we like in our great leaders.
Some days Hitler didn't kill anybody.

Even Geronimo, jaguar pussycat,
dozed in the sun sometimes. And a raging
sunspot that leaps for millions of miles
makes it a scorcher along our street
and ripens the corn.

In any town, or field, or forest,
or on the sea, wherever you are,
you may find a bird or fish, or maybe
a stray dog, to help. And that little act
will carry your name all the way to the stars.

By a River in the Osage Country

They called it Neosho, meaning
"a river made muddy by buffalo."
You don't need many words if you
already know what you're talking about,
and they did. But later there was
nothing they knew that made any difference.

I am thinking of those people—say one
of them looks at you; for an instant you see
a soul like your own, and you are both
lost. What the spirit has given
you to do is unworthy. Two kinds of
dirt, you look at each other.

But still, I have waded that river
and looked into the eyes of buffalo
that were standing and gazing far:
no soul I have met knew the source
that well, or where the Neosho
went when it was clear.

Wovoka in Nevada

Holding his dream (buffalo all over
the plains again, their generous gaze
topaz catching the sun) and then holding
the jewel his death, he went away.

Now you can walk on his dream and scatter
bottle caps kicked in the ditch. You can skip
out of the way when fast cars charge by
and their blind windshields dismiss you.

Or saved by money you can have a glittering town
and worship in a casino, bow to lights
and bells, pick up nickels near the railroad
crossing in Reno, and hear a soft reminder—

Wheels on the tracks going "Wovoka, Wovoka, Wovoka."

Arrival

While the years were mine I walked the high country
with a thought for a friend: *Somewhere, somewhere.*

And I heard the wind in its desperate quiet
smuggling winter through the dark forest.

I saw leaves massacred in autumn,
and their places taken by the stars at night.

In all the world no place was mine
because I was driven like the other things.

But then I found the tumbleweed secret,
bounding along saying, "Where is my home?"

And the voices began to come at night,
warning, "We're lost—don't be like us."

So when someone is near I reach out for them,
knowing how far it is when you're alone—

How out in space you finally accept
what has to be: *Anywhere, anywhere.*

Something I Was Thinking About

If anything ever happens to time again
let's crawl where we did that night in the cave
when both of us heard a star go by so still
that a crystal formed in our lives. Let's climb
that cavern the same slope as the hill but under
the hill, thus having the world as it is
but also shaped our way.

Don't answer me now, it's too early; but listen—
I'm just talking about this, but see
what you think, later, when you have time:
we could stand there together and hear day coming,
and we could be neutral but welcome what came.
We could bow and hear the far-off world
that we knew, going away.

Publius Vergilius Maro

Toward the last, paled by the page he wrote (eagles,
tan lions waiting for the Colosseum,
and Caesar determined that the claws
on his arm should lengthen Rome),
the writer suffered his whole picture of what
we are, a picture so adequate that we have become it.

Awed now, our leaders admire our kind
(the great works! the tremendous events
we create!) as—amazed by its portrait—
our mirror strains to believe its own depth,
or shatter what it is. Vergil, you saw,
deeper than war, these tears in human things:

That the blind in their dark have all they need.

Report from an Unappointed Committee

The uncounted are counting
    and the unseen are looking around.

In a room of northernmost light
    a sculptor named Ugly is making
    a strange opposite that is not beauty.

In some university a strict experiment
    has indicated a need for
    more strict experiments.

A wild confusion of order is clawing through
    a broken system of our most reliable wires.

In the farthest province a comet
    has flamed in the gaze of
    an unofficial watcher.

In the backcountry a random raindrop
    has broken a dam.

And a new river is out feeling for a valley
    somewhere under our world.

Santa's Workshop

The doll bodies glide past on little
wires that slide through their eyes.
They never meet—the boys and girls
turn a corner side by side and
enter a distant room to be boxed
separately. One at a time they are
released from the wires. Their eyes
rest. With folded arms they
take their place, lie down,
go out to save the world.

Seasons in the Country

1.

When we unfasten the cabin door in
the spring, an echo of our hammering
scares the blue jays, and all our section
of the country turns relevant for a while.

2.

Summer days have been falling thousands
of years; they land quietly in the woods
at dawn and come forward with an embrace
like light on old faces in the family album.

3.

Writing their history in the sky, the last
of the summer birds go away. We hear
empty woods bravely surround our house
in open ranks, for autumn census, unafraid.

4.

The storm that closes all the passes
just is—it doesn't come. It is as quiet
as in the story when the hunted wolf
wrestled with death in the hidden cave
      and nobody ever found out who won.

My Hands

It is time for applause. My hands rest
on the balcony railing. They inflict
their silence, lying there innocently.
Or—I may wound people by not shaking hands.
Somewhere a computer saves it up, my
indifference: if I ever meet the performer
our greeting will hover in the subtle gradations.

Sometimes I carry these weapons my hands
quietly to a reception. In their cuffs
they look tame, but I know them and hold them still.
When they pick up a glass or a sandwich they close
with just enough grip. They are generous,
always alert. And they're mine, terribly
sure, always loyal to me.

Our Journey, a Story from the Dust

Every town came true. Every person
stared. Hadn't they seen a boy before?
—and a little dog?—and a bear? It was miles for us,
mirages, heat, cold. We loved each other.
We had to find the North, where grandmothers told
about forest, rivers—old stories of bravery and friends,
how the world began. It was hundreds of miles. That long
road may never end: a boy, a little
dog, and a bear, in a story so true that still
this dust has to tell it like this again and again.

The Bush from Mongolia

This bush with light green leaves
came from Mongolia where
it learned everything about wind.

All day and all night that cold lesson
clawed its firm hands everywhere
over whatever dared live above the ground.

These branches will never reach out
and celebrate the sun; these roots
will not relax their hold on the rocks.

Some of us have to be ready—
the big winter can come back, and only
bushes from Mongolia will survive.

Fame

My book fell in a river and rolled
over and over turning its pages
for the sun. From a bridge I saw this.
An eagle dived and snatched the slippery volume.

Now somewhere in the forest that book, educating
eagles, turns its leaves in the wind,
and all those poems whisper for autumn
to come, and the long nights, and the snow.

Practice

When you stop off at rehearsal you can stumble
and still be forgiven. Your shadow practices. A light
says, "Good, good," where the piano meditates
with its wide grin, maintaining order as usual
but already trembling for time to go again.

Outside the hall a monstrous Oregon night
moans with its river of wind. It stumbles. Lights
flicker, and your shadow joins everything that ever
failed in the world, or triumphed unknown, alone,
wrapped in that secret mansion where genius lives.

Maybe it is all rehearsal, even when practice
ends and performance pretends to happen in the light
that remembers more than it touches, back through all
the rows and balcony tiers. Maybe your stumbling
saves you, and that sound in the night is more than the wind.

Maybe Alone on My Bike

I listen, and the mountain lakes
hear snowflakes come on those winter wings
only the owls are awake to see,
their radar gaze and furred ears
alert. In that stillness a meaning shakes;

And I have thought (maybe alone
on my bike, quaintly on a cold
evening pedaling home), Think!—
the splendor of our life, its current unknown
as those mountains, the scene no one sees.

O citizens of our great amnesty:
we might have died. We live. Marvels
coast by, great veers and swoops of air
so bright the lamps waver in tears,
and I hear in the chain a chuckle I like to hear.